Purr...

Children's Book Illustrators Brag about Their Cats

Edited by Michael J. Rosen

Harcourt Brace & Company

SAN DIEGO   NEW YORK   LONDON • PRINTED IN SINGAPORE

[contribu

tors]

15 VLADIMIR RADUNSKY
16 RODGER WILSON
17 PETER SIS
18 DIANE STANLEY
19 LESLIE BAKER
20 MARGARET BLOY GRAHAM
21 DYANNE DISALVO-RYAN
22 ROZ CHAST
23 NANCY WILLARD
24 WILL HILLENBRAND
25 EDWARD GOREY
26 JANE DYER
27 JANET STEVENS
28 PAUL MEISEL
29 GEORGE BOOTH

30 PETER HANNAN
31 ROXIE MUNRO
32 DAVID JOHNSON
33 DAVID DIAZ
34 DAVID BUTLER
35 ROBERT SABUDA
36 DAVID KIRK
37 JEANETTE WINTER
38 ROBERT ZIMMERMAN
39 AUDREY WOOD
40 DAVID MCPHAIL
41 STEVEN KELLOGG
42 TOM WHARTON

ENDPAPERS BY
ED YOUNG

PHOTOGRAPHY BY
DENNIS MOSNER

I like to brag about cats.

[i n t r o d u c t i o n]

Most people **I know like to brag about cats. But cats don't need all that flattery.** They already know that they're gorgeous and aristocratic, that they're gifted dancers, great batters, admirable vocalists, and accomplished acrobats. We can brag all we want about our cats and they'll just go on doing whatever they've been doing, because cats are really self-employed and don't care if they please the boss or not.

Cats never brag about their people, though they do have complaints. Mrow . . . you're late with the food. Mrow . . . why haven't you opened the curtains yet? Mrow . . . how come I can't

go outside today? Cats have a lot to say and not very much of it is complimentary. A happy cat is a quiet cat, basking in the sun, playing with something little that moves, purring softly in someone's lap.

You might remember from an earlier book called *SPEAK! Children's Book Illustrators Brag about Their Dogs,* that I have two retrievers in my family who, like most dogs, appreciate flattery just as people do. But we have no cats. It's not that Paris and Madison couldn't learn to get along with cats. In fact, they did once. Here's a picture of a tiny

kitten with my dogs. We found him, a six-week-old kitten strolling down Long Street among the speeding cars. He was one of the million kittens born to stray cats each year who are likely to never find a home. But we snatched him up and brought him to our house.

My dogs were very concerned with this wobbly creature. After a thorough two-nose inspection, Paris and Madison gave him a head-to-toe licking. Though cleaner from the bath, the kitten looked like a wrung-out washcloth. Finally, tired and hungry, the kitten snuggled up to Paris, the golden retriever, and began to knead with his front paws and poke his nose at my dog's side. Paris didn't move, but he also couldn't tell the little guy that not only was his new mother a dog, she was a male dog at that.

I mashed a little leftover crab cake into some milk and made a phone call. Even before the kitten could finish my first attempt at kitty-food chowder,

my friend Susan arrived, named him Tinker, and whisked him away, cuddled inside her sweater, to his new home.

Although we've gone to visit Tinker, he doesn't remember Paris and Madison fondly. At least, he doesn't act as if he wants to snuggle or have another two-dog bath.

So it's not the dogs' fault that we don't have cats. The problem is that I'm allergic to Tinker and to every other cat I've ever met. But that doesn't keep me from doting on my favorite ones. Like Spanky, who spends a part of every day atop my pal Jennifer's

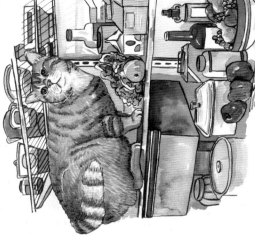

aquarium,
guarding her solitary fish. He seems very proud of his job. (Maybe he also likes the humming warmth of the pump and heater beneath the lid.)

Or like Magoo, whose favorite place in his apartment happens to be inside the refrigerator. Of course, he can only explore the cold box for as long as my friend Debbie is deciding on what she needs for cooking.

And then there's Jennie's cat, Virgil, who spends most summer afternoons on the screened-in porch dreaming of birds—at least he flaps his paws as if he's flying after birds in his dreams.

I know other lucky cats, too, like the ones collected here—cats who share the safety and comfort of someone's home. I also know there are a lot of unlucky cats in this world—cats who never find homes. Because you have this book in your hands, you are helping to feed a community of stray cats, find a home for an unwanted litter, or give a kitten the medical care some family couldn't afford. Profits from this book, as well as

from several others I have edited, are undoing a little of the human carelessness that has brought so many unwanted pets into our overcrowded world. More than 250 artists and writers have helped in these collections, each of them donating work so

that, together, as The Company of Animals Fund, we can offer grants to animal welfare agencies around the country. I guess that's something to brag about.

On behalf of all those luckier animals we are helping, I thank you. And on behalf of all those who still need our help, I hope your kindness will extend far beyond this book.

Now, on with the bragging!

[m o u s e   &   w i l l i e]

ONE IS A furry gray-and-
white blob nested in a round
cat bed. The other is a little
tabby curled in a C without
a care to be seen.
Catnapping, kitty dozing,
dreaming purrfect dreams—
Mooshky Mouse and Bobcat
Willie remind us that cats
have the answer we will
probably never know.

A FINE lap-and-couch cat, Beano was also an excellent hunter and bold adventurer. At night she slept in the back of my old Corvair or among the socks and shirts in the laundry-chute box. During the day, she perched on the air conditioner outside the kitchen window, where she could listen for the electric can opener inside as well as keep watch on her neighborhood.

One day a pack of dogs spotted her on the air conditioner and ran straight toward her. We heard the commotion and dashed outside, but Beano didn't need our help. She rode the back of the biggest dog, clinging with her claws all the way to the end of the driveway, where she dismounted. Then she trotted proudly back to the house, hopped onto the air conditioner, and freshened up—all that dog smell!

2

[b e a n o]

[n u t k i n]

NUTKIN HAS a web of secret
paths among the complex of
barns and outbuildings on
Clipper Ship Farm.

Though I see him grooming
his coat in the sunny
cabbage patch, I like to
imagine Nutkin at night,
crouching behind those
cabbages to watch an owl
pursue a field mouse.

Though I see him tight-
roping the rickety fence
between hay barn and
toolshed, I like to imagine

him, just before dawn,
balancing on the roof's
peak for the best view of
the rising sun.

And though I see him
sleeping in the children's
beds, on a cushion near
the woodstove, and behind
a bale of hay, my favorite
way to imagine Nutkin—
especially when the
neighborhood car alarms are
keeping me awake—is
sound asleep in a nesting
box among the chickens.

DURING THE day, Vincent works as an excellent thermometer:

40°

50°

60°

70°

80°

90°

100°

[v i n c e n t]

At night he swipes a bathroom towel and rides it at a high rate of speed over town. He has *never* lost his hat.

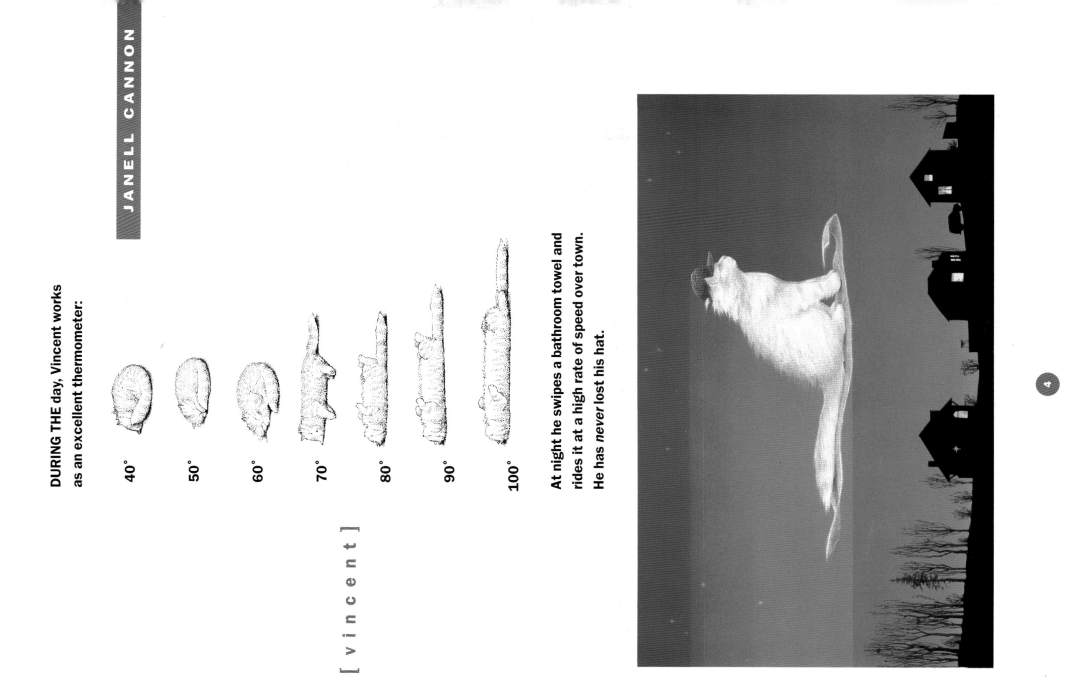

LIZZY WAS a thinker. Not in the philosophical sense. She mostly thought everyday kinds of thoughts, like how to get in and out of the house. For this we provided her with her own little door. Kneeling at the basement door, we tried to teach her—"Through the flap, OUT! IN! OUT! IN!"

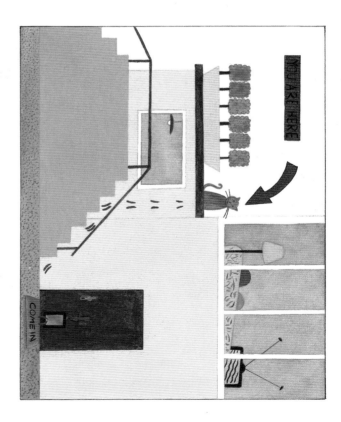

YOU ARE HERE

COME IN

After a few weeks she caught on. This became the foundation for our daily ritual. When she was in and saw us out, she wanted out. When she was out and saw us in, she wanted in. She would watch us through the window. Eventually, a glazed look would come over her. "I know there is a way," she'd think. Many minutes later she'd join us. "She made it," I'd say. "Clever Lizzy," my husband would say, lifting her onto his shoulder.

Now Lizzy is in heaven; no doors, no flaps, but she carries a compass in her purse.

[l i z z y]

5

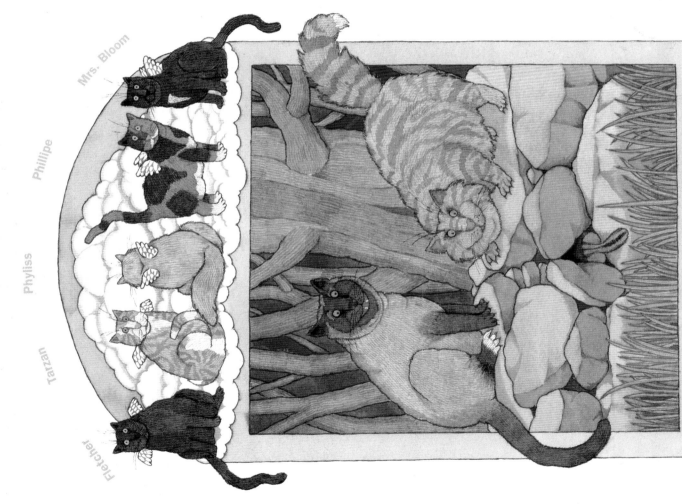

Mrs. Bloom

Phillipe

Phyliss

Tarzan

Fletcher

[z a z o u & p e a r l]

IT'S NOT possible to think of the cats who are with you now without thinking of the cats who were with you before. They overlap like the seasons.

Currently, Zazou and Pearl are in residence. Zazou won our hearts with her extraordinarily messy appearance and her fondness for being held upside down.

Pearl was abandoned near our house. Sensing that she might not be wanted, she immediately proved herself essential: She disposed of six brown rats in our basement and took to greeting guests with all the grace of a cocktail waitress.

Zazou and Pearl loathe each other. Only sometimes do they operate in tandem. They catch chipmunks, sneak them through the door, and release them near the chunky bullterrier. After a satisfying explosion of dog and an upheaval of furniture, the cats congratulate each other.

VICTORIA CHESS

MY MOM didn't allow us to have cats when we were kids. They scratched the furniture. That was OK, though, because I had a tiger. An African tiger. He was orange with black stripes and piercing teeth.

JOHN SEGAL

7

Naturally, he had to stay in my room during the day. Dad was concerned that if Tiger were free to roam the yard, he might get loose one day and eat the neighbor's weebok.

But at night, when everyone else had gone to sleep, Tiger's day would begin. Sometimes I'd go with him. He'd let me ride on his back. Together we'd wander the savanna until dawn, then we'd sneak back into the house. And as I'd brush my teeth and get ready for school, Tiger would go to sleep.

AJ is a saint.

He doesn't go around scratching up the whole house like most cats. He only claws the nice couch. When it comes to eating, seven meals a day are more than enough for our frugal feline. And who needs a rooster? We have the best little waker-upper in all of New York City. Every morning right at five A.M.

What a saint. What a cat!

[a j]

ERICK INGRAHAM

[h e n r y]

I HAVE maintained as many as six cats at the same time, but in 1977 a certain cat entered my life. Ever since then, I've been overshadowed by his immortal presence.

[wendy & groucho]

IT IS NOW two months since we introduced Wendy the kitten to our fourteen-year-old Burmese, Groucho. Wendy has the upper hand. She runs about where she wants to, poops in Groucho's private litter, and sleeps near him (though she's careful not to touch him).

Even if Groucho seems to have lost something of his self-esteem, in the mornings he moves his arthritic legs fast enough to catch Wendy. And maybe that's enough. A little aerobics in the morning and a more or less uninterrupted snooze all afternoon.

JAMES McMULLAN

10

[s y l]

SYL, SYL, the Unpleasant Cat:
Everyone loves to describe you like that.
Is it due to your permanent scowl and your sneer,
Which is caused by a tooth that's been missing for years?

Syl, Syl, the Cat We All Hate,
How is it you come by this unloving fate
That even the kindest of people all chide:
"Please shut up that cat and throw him outside."

Syl, Syl, I'm afraid I must say
That most of the time I do wish you'd go 'way.
Yet I have to admit you keep the place free
Of vermin and pests (and without DDT!).

And if I had my wish, could I deal with that?
Wouldn't I miss my horrible cat?
The truth is, My Kitty, My Syl, and My Joy,
You live with an equally Unpleasant Boy.

WARD SCHUMAKER

JUST AFTER World War II, my favourite uncle, Barry, lived in a beautiful, furnitureless flat in London. The lights were on again, but food was still scarce.

Barry was given a kitten, a pretty white thing named Snowy. I was visiting one day, and we put Snowy out onto the balcony to play. Suddenly, the tiny kitten backed into the room, dragging a huge steak.

After a small struggle, Barry won the steak and cleaned it under the tap. Delicious! But where had the steak come from? The balcony was four floors above the street, and there were no others within a cat's jump. "Doesn't do to inquire!" said Barry. "The Lord will always provide."

Not so, because although Lord Snowy was put out onto the balcony every day for a month, the cheated aristocrat provided no more steak.

SMUDGE TV. That's what we call it every time we see our cat, Smudge, staring out the window.

"Would you like to go out, Smudge?" we ask. "It's too nice to be inside." (We like to sound just like our parents used to sound when we wanted to play indoors.)

Blink. Blink. Smudge just stares out the window. "Ow," she says.

"What's on TV tonight, Smudge?"

"Ow."

Maybe life's hard with only one channel.

[c l a y]

MONA LISA's smile is not just a mouth that
turns up at the corners. Her whole face
glows in quiet satisfaction. When I watch
Clay, my cat, I see the same satisfied smile.
In fact, Mona Lisa looks to me like the cat
that swallowed the canary.

[f e d o r a]

HERE'S a man
Who lost his hat.
Here's a cat
Who's sympathetic to that.

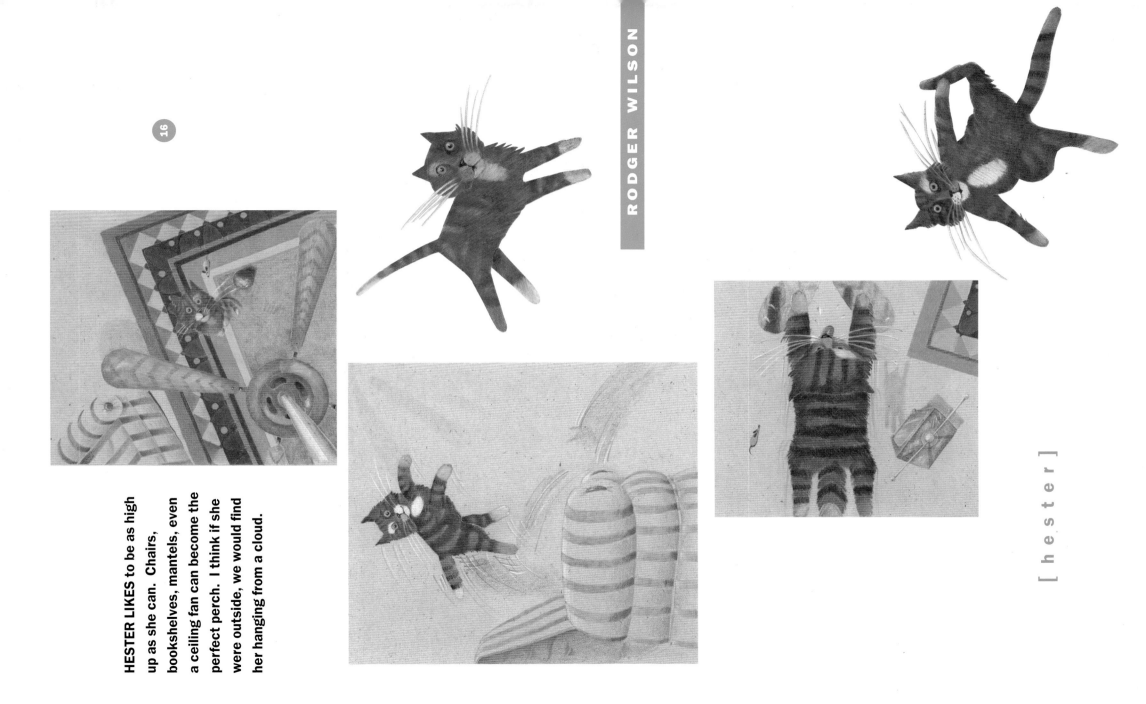

HESTER LIKES to be as high up as she can. Chairs, bookshelves, mantels, even a ceiling fan can become the perfect perch. I think if she were outside, we would find her hanging from a cloud.

[h e s t e r]

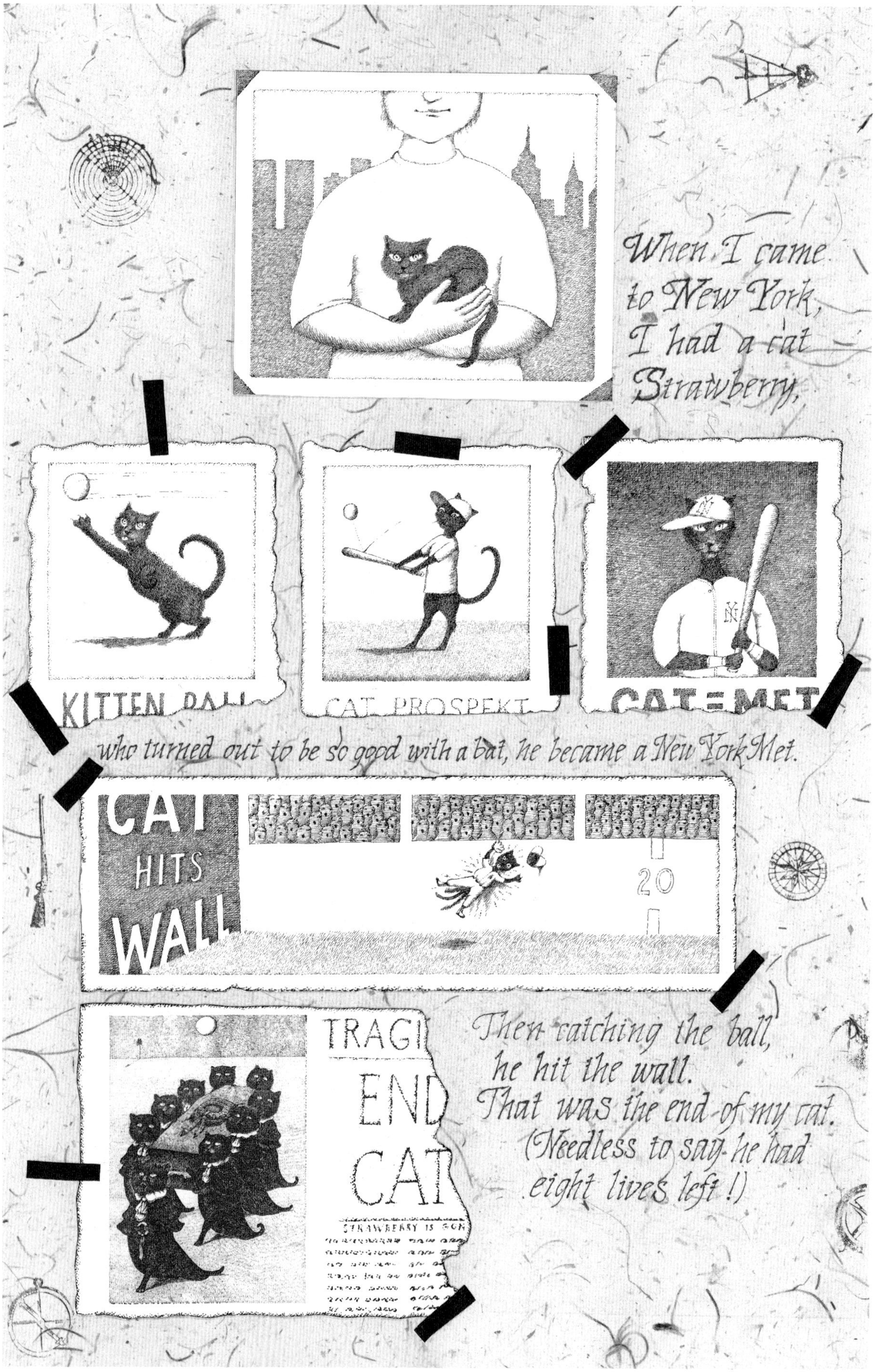

When I came to New York, I had a cat Strawberry,

who turned out to be so good with a bat, he became a New York Met.

KITTEN BALL

CAT PROSPEKT

CATS MET

CAT HITS WALL

20

TRAGIC END CAT

Then watching the ball,
he hit the wall.
That was the end of my cat.
(Needless to say, he had
eight lives left.)

EARLY ONE Saturday
morning my daughter
whispered into my ear,
"Mom, there's a cat having
kittens in our laundry room."
That woke me up!

She had gone out for a
walk, and the cat had just
"followed her home."
Tamara is allergic to cats,
but what did that matter
when faced with a damsel
in distress? So mama kitty
and her five babies got a
cozy nest, a kitty feast,
and far too much attention.

About a week later the
books on my bookshelf
began to call out to me.
They said, "Mew." I pulled
the loudest book off the
shelf, and there behind it
sat two kittens. As I stood
there amazed, along came
mama kitty with a third baby
in her mouth. She wanted to
raise her family with a little
privacy, please! Or maybe,
like a wise mother, she just
thought an early exposure
to books would be good
for them.

[a damsel in distress]

[n e l l i e]

NELLIE IS a city feline whose greatest pleasure is staring out my third-floor studio windows at the birds and squirrels in nearby trees. But whenever she gets the chance she escapes, eliciting a round of frantic calls from concerned neighbors because she likes to tightrope walk along the rooftop edges of the town houses. She always finds her way home, however, and always in time for meals.

[l u c y]

LUCY IS fifteen years old and loves to sleep: on the furnace, on my desk, in a drawer, in my closet, and on my bed—wherever it's warm.

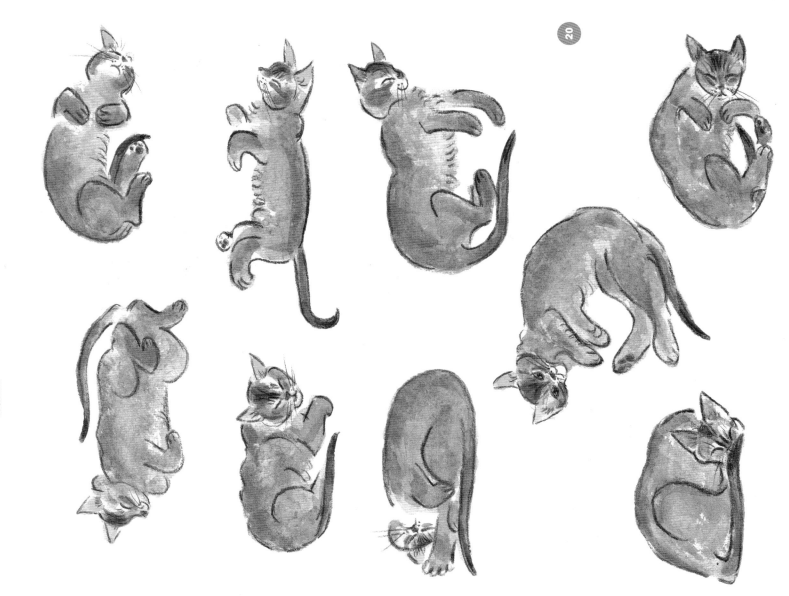

[s c a r e d y   k a t e]

SCAREDY KATE is a plump calico. She became "scaredy" on the day three blue jays spotted her under a cherry tree and chased her all the way home. Scaredy Kate had her first and only litter of kittens on Father's Day, and bore them in the corner of my husband's closet surrounded by his sneakers. We called them his Father's Day presents, and named the kittens Adidas, Nike, Converse, Etonic, and Reebok.

[h a r r i e t]

I used to have a cat who was crazy about Super Balls — those little balls that bounce really, really high.

I'd throw about ten at a time and watch her go into a frenzy chasing and retrieving them.

Over time, however, those balls would disappear, one by one. Laziness kept me from doing a real thorough search — I'd just go out and buy some more.

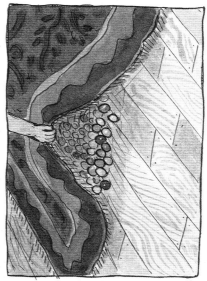

They must be here somewhere.

One day, I was in a thrifty, industrious mood. I decided to hunt for those "lost" Super Balls. It was a one-room apartment, so it wasn't as if there were limitless hiding places.

I tore the place apart, with no luck. Finally, I decided that they had all vanished into the infamous Lost Cat Toy dimension, and gave up.

About a year later, while packing to move, I happened to lift up an obscure, wedged-in section of carpet and hit pay dirt: 42 BALLS.

ROZ CHAST

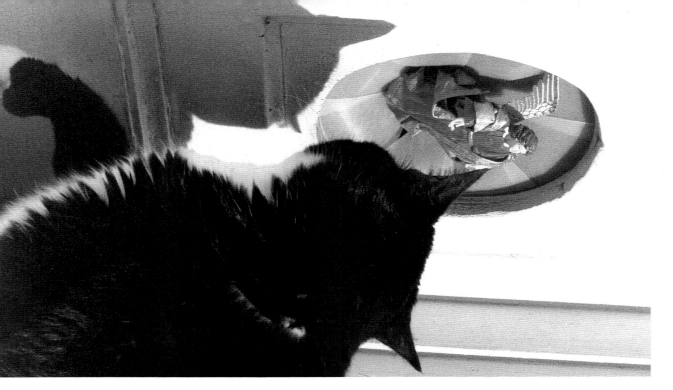

[t h u m b s]

23

O, SIX-TOED CAT, forgive us
for naming you Thumbs.

The field mice call you
Full Moon Eyes Sweeping the Dark.
The moles call you
He Who Hears Footsteps under the Earth.
The bats call you Steeple Ears.
The frogs call you
He Whose Paw Scoops the
         Moon from Mud Puddles.

The five-toed cats call you
Meow of Meows,
Most Magical Majesty,
Cousin of Tiger,
Godchild of Lion.
Paw-Crusher,
         Neck-Biter,
              Wing-Chomper,
Most Merciful Seer
who saw an angel and let it pass.

[b u d d y / m i s s y]

OUR CAT WAS the only pet who came to us by way of our back door. He looked hungry, so Mom made him a little snack. . . . The cat stayed (who could blame him?) and we adopted him. He was already full grown and certainly friendly; we named him Buddy. Buddy was the center of attention for weeks, but then, as suddenly as he had entered our lives, he was gone. We got our flashlights and sent out search parties. After hunting for days and days, we gave up hope and feared the worst. Two weeks later we once again heard something at our back door. We were elated to discover that it was Buddy! And four tiny kittens were with him— with her, I mean. So we changed Buddy's name to Missy and named one of the kittens Buddy instead.

WILL HILLENBRAND

[h e n r y]

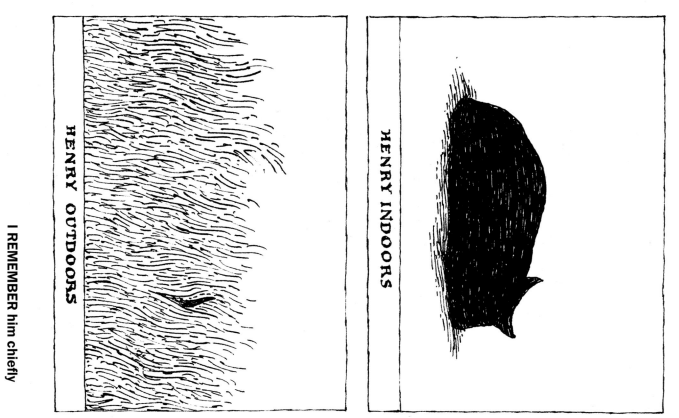

HENRY INDOORS

HENRY OUTDOORS

I REMEMBER him chiefly
As very large and black
And forbiddingly serious;
I knew him only briefly
Before he did not come back,
His end mysterious.

[t u x e d o]

WHEN I was seven, I wrote a poem about my constant companion, Tux:

I have a cat,
Tuxedo by name.
He looks quite mean
But he's really
very tame.

I had always wanted a pretty cat. And although Tux was pretty ugly, I loved him just the same. Worse than ugly, he was a big bully, always fighting with other cats.

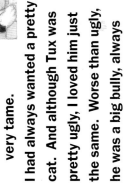

I did my best to help him improve himself. I dressed him in nice clothes and conducted daily lessons to teach him reading and writing. To refine his social graces and to help him make friends, I arranged small gatherings and invited the neighborhood pets. On his second birthday I threw a party and invited

a beagle, kitten, rabbit, goldfish, and parakeet. But his manners didn't improve: Even before it was time to unwrap presents, Tux opened all the gifts containing catnip.

Poor Merlin is too fat to fit on this page!

[merlin]

27

PATIENCE WAS not high on the list of Max's virtues. When he wanted to go outside, Max would look my father straight in the eye and shred a piece of furniture. Replacing furniture was not high on my father's list of priorities. Max was let outside in a hurry.

[m a x]

28

In the middle of the night, Max's routine differed slightly. Fifteen, or maybe thirty, seconds of carpet shredding roused my father from the soundest sleep. I guess you could say persistence might have been high on Max's list of virtues: When he wanted out, he truly wanted out.

GEORGE BOOTH

ONCE UPON a limb in a walnut tree
there resided a Pussycat
in an abandoned squirrel's nest.

Down below in the hollow trunk
lived a spotted neighbor
who howled all night.

All night at the moon. Oh!
Pussycat never could sleep.
Never could sleep.

Pussycat thought that perhaps,
perhaps, her spotted neighbor
who howls at the moon

would like a gift from a Pussycat?
Perhaps a nice green walnut?
Pussycat selected a nice green walnut.

A nice green walnut.
Um-hum.
And sent it to her spotted neighbor.

The spotted neighbor was so pleased
with the gift of a nice green walnut
that he stopped howling at the moon.

And Pussycat who
lived in an abandoned squirrel's nest
snatched a little bit of shut-eye. Happily.

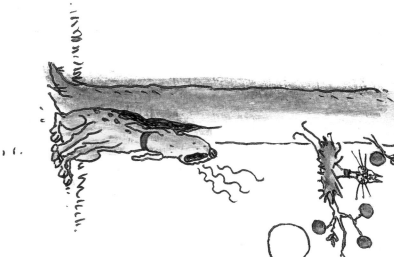